God's Golden Vision

Peter Scothern

New Wine Press

New Wine Press
PO Box 17
Chichester
PO20 6YB
England

Bible references are from the Authorised Version.

ISBN 1 903725 06 2

Typeset by CRB Associates, Reepham, Norfolk.
Printed in England by Clays Ltd, St Ives plc.

Contents

Foreword

I have known Peter Scothern for 34 years and both my wife and I have been greatly blessed by his Christ-centred ministry of preaching the full gospel which has been confirmed with 'signs and wonders' in the power of the Spirit of God.

Both my wife and I have been healed from serious illnesses by the Lord through the prayers and encouragement given by Peter and the faithful Christians we have come to know and love through coming into contact with him.

If you have ever wondered about God's overall plan for your life, this book is for you, since it traces how God has, and is making provision for you both in this life and for eternity.

When God created the earth and mankind He foresaw all that would happen and how His perfect creation would be corrupted by the sin which entered the world through the disobedience of Adam.

By the time of Noah evil had increased to such an extent that God decided to make an end to mankind by the means of the world-wide flood. He did, however, make provision for Noah and his family who both trusted and obeyed Him. Jesus Christ makes it clear that exactly the same evil conditions will occur again on the earth when He returns, and as for Noah so will He make provision for those who trust and obey Him. We love a righteous and merciful God who patiently waits for every person to decide whether or not to accept His offer of a life shared with Him. For those who accept the future is bright, since, apart from the joy of being delivered from our sinful nature, we have the promise that we will reign with Him when He returns to the earth.

If we are to receive the inheritance which God has prepared for us, the Lord makes it clear to St John in Revelation that it is those who 'over-come' in this world who will receive the promise of the 'New Jerusalem'. St Paul describes this state as being 'incorruptible and undefiled' – one which remains for ever. This can only be obtained through a God-given faith, the mystery of which we will probably not completely understand until we see Him face-to-face.

David Way
July 2001
Pastor, The People's Mission Church, Bath

Chapter 1

God's Golden Vision

The opening chapter of the book of Genesis portrays our planet earth as a unique creation.

Verse one states:

> *In the beginning God created the heaven and the earth.'* (Genesis 1:1)

This clear and concise statement places the creation of the earth alongside the creation of heaven; both creations being specifically listed with a divine vision and purpose. The earth is indeed a unique creation. No other planet in our solar system compares with it. First, we are informed the earth was originally covered with water. The present seas and oceans bear testimony to this. Every effort is being made to discover water somewhere in the universe with fragile success. This makes the earth unique. Secondly, this earth is furnished with such exquisite elements that it is ideal for human habitation. In fact, if only one of these vital elements went missing – e.g. light, water, air – the human race would cease to exist. This unique planet, according to Genesis 1:14–19, existed before our solar system. It was on the **fourth day** of creation we read:

> '*God made two great lights* [sun, moon]; *the greater light to rule the day, and the lesser light to rule the night: he made the stars also ... And the evening and the morning were the* **fourth day**.'
>
> (Genesis 1:16, 19)

It is also obvious that planet earth is an ideal location for humankind designed and created by a **divine mastermind**. This being so, the earth must play an important role in God's divine purpose. It is the stage upon which the drama of the human race is being enacted. As we consider each act of this human drama we will begin to focus upon **God's golden vision** and learn some of the secrets of His divine mind.

Man – a unique creation

> '*And God said, Let the earth bring forth the living creature after his kind, cattle, and creeping thing, and beast of the earth after his kind: and it was so ... And God said, Let us make man in our image, after our likeness: and let them have dominion ... over all the earth and over every creeping thing that creepeth upon the earth. So God created man in his own image, in the image of God created he him; male and female created he them.*'
>
> (Genesis 1:24, 26–27)

As sure as the earth is a unique creation so is humankind. There is no creation throughout the solar system to compare with mankind. Mankind is a miracle of the highest order. Consider just one aspect of the human body – e.g. the blood content and the following documented statistics reveal the uniqueness of the human creation.

The average adult weighing 11–12 stones has around 10 pints of blood. This contains **30 million white blood cells** to help cleanse and purify the body, fight disease and carry away waste products. There are **100 trillion red blood cells** to carry oxygen and food to the body, and also to keep the body at the correct temperature. Other ingredients include platelets and plasma, the latter being a straw-coloured liquid comprising 55% of the blood content. Our bodies contain 1,000 miles of main arteries and veins plus 100,000 miles of blood vessels – sufficient to encircle the world four times. Our hearts are the pumping stations. They beat on average 70 times per minute – 4,200 times every hour. That is 100,000 times daily or **2 billion** times in 70 years. The heart lifts 500,000 tons of blood during an average life span which equals a tanker train over 40 miles in length. Such amazing statistics prove beyond question the uniqueness of man.

- The earth is a unique creation!
- Mankind is a unique creation!

Therefore, the divine reason for the existence of the earth and mankind must also be unique. Hence the title of this book – *God's Golden Vision*.

Created in God's image

Return to Genesis 1:24–27: '*And God said, let us*

make man in our image, after our likeness: and let them have dominion...' (v. 26). In simple, concise language God shares with us the reason and purpose for His creation of mankind. To thoroughly investigate exactly what God meant when He stated *in our image, after our likeness'* will take a lifetime to explore. And yet in this initial declaration God does reveal His desire to create mankind **after His likeness**. Also we can presume with confidence that **the end product of this process** will be pleasing to the Lord. For it is certain that in order to become like God's image a tremendous transformation will have to occur over a period of time. Analysing humanity's present state in body, soul, and mind it falls exceedingly short of God's image. When the God of creation presented to the world His only begotten Son, Jesus Christ, mankind soon realised there is an impassable gulf between sinful humanity and the holy, immaculate Son of God. So how did God propose to bridge this gulf and bring His purposes to fruition?

The divine process

This divine process was revealed to mankind in distinct stages. The Lord God is omniscient, i.e. all knowing – all knowledge, knowing past, present and future. When He created Adam and Eve He placed them in the garden of Eden. This was a perfect and ideal environment.

> *'And the LORD God planted a garden eastward in Eden; and there he put the man whom he had*

formed. And out of the ground made the LORD God to grow every tree that is pleasant to the sight, and good for food.' (Genesis 2:8–9)

God, in His foreknowledge was fully aware of the dramatic events that would befall Adam and Eve. He was not taken by surprise by the tragedy that followed. The apostle Paul highlights this issue in his illuminating epistle to the Romans:

*'For the creature was made subject to vanity, **not willingly**, but **by reason of him** who hath **subjected** the same in hope. Because the creature itself also **shall be delivered from the bondage of corruption into the glorious liberty of the children of God.'*** (Romans 8:20–21)

The apostle here makes clear God's divine intention to fulfil His pledge – 'to make man after His image and likeness'.

Garden of Eden drama

The Garden of Eden drama, in the light of Paul's revelation was part of the vision and purpose of God. The Lord allowed Satan to become the instrument of evil but even this rebellious action did not deter God from proceeding with His ultimate vision and purpose.

Of course, a burning question could arise at this point: 'What was God's reason for allowing sin into the world?' I can assure you this is a question that has occupied my heart and mind over many years. Bear in mind that the **sin** problem is much older than the human race and the Garden of Eden event.

11

The writer to the Hebrews gives light on this mysterious subject. He informs us that the shed blood of Christ was necessary for the cleansing of the heavens as well as the earth.

> *'It was therefore necessary that the patterns of things in the **heavens** should be purified with these; but the heavenly things themselves with better sacrifices than these.'*   (Hebrews 9:23)

What had transpired in the heavens to contaminate the place? A rebellious cherub, named Gadreel (Satan) had aspired to rise up against the Most High. Satan and the angels who supported this rebellion were justly excommunicated from heaven. They were cast out but continued their evil activities whenever the opportunity arose. According to the Genesis record, Satan (meaning God's enemy), appeared in the Garden of Eden seducing the serpent before deceiving Adam and Eve. Through this evil intervention **sin** entered the human race.

A similar happening occurred in the days of Noah. According to Enoch the prophet, 200 fallen angels visited the earth causing havoc and confusion. The resulting evil proved so intense that God terminated humankind with flood water saving only eight righteous souls. The apostle Peter makes mention of this traumatic event in his epistle:

> *'For if God spared not **the angels that sinned**, but cast them down to hell, and delivered them into chains of darkness, to be **reserved unto judgment**; And spared not the old world, but saved Noah the eighth person, a preacher of*

righteousness, bringing in the flood upon the world of the ungodly.'   (2 Peter 2:4–5)

And yet, in spite of each satanic intrusion, God forged ahead with His long-term purpose. Nothing would deter Him from reaching His goal to 'make man after His likeness and image'. He was determined to proceed with His **golden vision**.

The faithful devotees

Throughout the early history of God's dealings with mankind there were dedicated devotees who were willing to pay the price and accompany God with His divine purpose. The Old Testament tells us of Enoch, Noah, Abraham, Jacob, Moses, and other faithful patriarchs who covenanted with the Lord God to crusade for the divine vision. While the worldlings pursued their independent and oft-times sinful ways these loyal devotees chose to follow the ways of the Lord.

Part of the process was to introduce the practice of covenant sacrifice accompanied by divine laws, creeds and commandments. The ten commandments revealed to Moses on Mount Sinai were typical conditions set forth by the Lord God to the elect nation of Israel. Strict obedience to the divine commandments was ordered by the Lord. Those who obeyed were divinely blessed but those who disobeyed were blighted.

The divine process

Each ongoing dispensation introduced some new encouragement in the divine process 'to make man after our image'. The tabernacle provided the sacrificial rites for the atonement for sin; the word 'atonement' meaning 'covering for sin'. This divinely instituted provision enabled God to fellowship with man in visible and audible ways. The priesthood was chosen and elected by God to act as mediator between sinful humanity and the Lord God of heaven. God was able to reveal in more detailed terms the vision dear to His heart.

The apostle Paul commends Abraham who implicitly obeyed God. 'Abraham's faith being counted for righteousness'; applied righteousness certainly proving a step in the right direction. Moses was also personally involved in discussion with the Lord God revealing such a dialogue was now possible. Gradually and wisely the Lord was progressing with His ultimate vision to *make man in our image'*.

The Son of God

When God sent His only begotten Son, Jesus, miraculously born of a virgin, He presented to the human race 'the image' He had so long envisaged. Jesus in the flesh was God's ideal image for mankind. Jesus was the first human that matched God's ultimate likeness. This perfect man was the prototype of all the human sons of God and those longing and yearning to be part of God's golden future were now able to visualize their ultimate goal.

Having presented the perfect man, God then provided the grace and means to become like Him. The act of atonement (covering for sin) was replaced by the remission of sin; Jesus, of His own will, bearing our sins in Himself at Calvary. The iron-fisted authority of sin was finally broken, the blood of Jesus providing the perfect antidote for the sin problem. Under the law dispensation mankind was obligated by his own discipline and ingenuity to obey every letter and precept. Under the dispensation of grace God would provide the grace and power for sinners to become the sons of God.

Participation not imitation

Before I introduce the steps Jesus outlines in the New Testament to fulfil God's golden vision, let me emphasise one important factor. We will never be conformed to the image of God's Son by **imitation**, i.e. striving in our own strength to copy Jesus. Simply to **copy Christ's life and methods** is not the answer. Imitation, however zealously applied, must yield to **participation**. Only the inward workings of the Holy Spirit can accomplish this divine purpose. The living Christ must be resident *in* **our lives** to bring about the transformation to be changed into His image.

Merely striving to live like a Christian is far beneath the meaning of eternal truth. The very reason for living is Christ Himself. His presence, power and Spirit indwelling our lives is absolutely essential for God's golden vision. To comply with the divine conditions of sonship, we must prayerfully consider the following scriptural steps with an ardent desire to obey them.

Chapter 2

You *Must* Be Born Again

A legend perpetuated by tourist guides in Nazareth tells how the virgin Mary was collecting water from the communal well when she was confronted by the angel Gabriel. Having visited the city on many occasions I find this location an ideal setting for one of God's most amazing appointments. At Nazareth the all-wise Lord of the universe set in motion an ingenious plan to transform sinful mankind into the sons of the living God. The coming of Christ into this world, endowed with divine nature but clothed in humanity, is assuredly the central enigma of the incarnation.

> *'God was in Christ, reconciling the world unto himself.'* (2 Corinthians 5:19)

Take careful note of the divine procedure.

Virgin with child

Upon hearing from Gabriel the virgin Mary would bear a son, she questioned,

'How shall this be, seeing I know not a man?'
(Luke 1:34)

The angel answered and said unto her:

'The Holy Ghost shall come upon thee, and the power of the Highest shall overshadow thee: therefore also that holy thing which shall be born of thee shall be called the Son of God.' (Luke 1:35)

This unprecedented event fulfilled an earlier prediction by Isaiah the prophet:

'Therefore the Lord himself shall give you a sign; Behold, a virgin shall conceive, and bear a son, and shall call his name Immanuel [God with us].*'*
(Isaiah 7:14)

- The Christ-child was **conceived by the Holy Ghost.**
- His divine life and nature came from heaven (John 8:23).
- His divine spirit was pure and free from sin.
- His physical body was after the natural order.
- It pleased God to send His only begotten Son in human form.
- His spirit was without spot or blemish.
- His body subject to the same temptations as ours.

Like unto Ark of the Covenant

The old testament Ark of the Covenant symbolized the coming of Christ. The pure golden upper section containing the cherubim represented **the deity** of Christ, i.e. His status as the Son of God. The lower section made of wood represented **His humanity**, i.e. His standing as the Son of Man.

The nature and life of Jesus came from His Father (John 16:28).

> *'For as the Father hath life in himself: so hath he given to the Son to have life in himself.'*
>
> (John 5:26)

I have emphasised this remarkable fact for a special reason.

Turn to John chapter 3 and diligently consider the following statements from Christ:

> *'Verily, verily, I say unto thee, Except a man be born again, he cannot see the Kingdom of God.'*
>
> (John 3:3)

> *'Verily, verily, I say unto thee, Except a man be born of water* [natural birth] *and of the Spirit* [second birth], *he cannot enter the Kingdom of God.'*
>
> (John 3:5)

> *'Marvel not that I said unto thee, **Ye must be born again**.'*
>
> (John 3:7)

An absolute necessity

The born-again experience is an absolute necessity, according to Jesus.

Without the new birth it is neither possible to see nor enter the Kingdom of God. We **must** be born again!

What is this **new birth** experience? What does it mean to be 'born again'?

- Our first birth is after the natural order: the second birth is a spiritual experience.
- Our first birth inherits the fallen nature of our human father: the second birth inherits the life and nature of the risen Christ.
- Our first birth is of corruptible seed: the second birth is of incorruptible seed.
- To be born again is to be spiritually reborn from above.
- It is the implanting by the blessed Holy Spirit of the very nature and life of Jesus.
- It is receiving a new spiritual life impacting our inner self, resulting in a spiritual and moral transformation.
- Our sin infected lives must be transformed by the injection of a **new life** and a **divine nature**.

This is exactly what Jesus prescribed two thousand years ago by saying we must be reborn from above. We cannot change or purify our sin tainted natures.

Some are enslaved by sinful habits they cannot break. Others are helpless victims to unclean conversations, evil actions and deeds.

In fact we have all sinned to some degree and come short of the glory of God.

Simply becoming religious and self-righteous will not overcome the problem of our sin-contaminated natures.

We **must be born again** by the Spirit of God.

The incoming and indwelling of the Christ life will result in a miraculous transformation of the way we talk, walk and live. We will be completely changed from within. The new birth will put us in touch with heaven and completely change our lifestyle and destiny.

Jesus will become a reality with His peace and presence filling our souls.

Reader, **have you been born again?**

Chapter 3

How to Be Born Again

Step No. 1
Recognize your need to receive the Christ life and nature. Be determined to start afresh and begin a new relationship with the risen Lord. Turn your back on all that is dubious, insincere and unholy.

Step No. 2
Confess your faults and failings to God. Be frank and open with Him. Request His help to remove your sinful ways. Consider Christ's crucifixion. Remember Jesus died bearing your sins in His body on the cross (1 Peter 2:24).

Step No. 3
Humbly and sincerely ask for God's divine forgiveness. Desire the cleansing of your life. God has promised, 'if we confess our sin, He is faithful and just to forgive us and cleanse us through the blood of Jesus, His Son' (1 John 1:9).

Believe God loves you and forgives you. Show your appreciation by giving thanks.

Step No. 4

Open your heart and mind to Christ's indwelling presence. Invite the living, risen Jesus into your life. Surrender yourself to His will and purpose. Jesus stands at the door of your life (Revelation 3:20). Open the door and bid Him welcome.

Step No. 5

Read Romans 10:9 and act upon it. Confess with your mouth that you have received Christ into your life. Do not be ashamed to identify with the most wonderful person in the universe. Other born-again Christians will support and assist you. Fellowship with them.

Step No. 6

Read your Bible daily beginning with the gospel of St John in the New Testament. Talk with God regularly through prayer and communion. Join in fellowship with other Christians who show a genuine desire to walk with God. Delight yourself in the Lord and seek to obey His commandments. Do not be afraid of ridicule or opposition. Pray for those who do not understand the reason why you love and serve the Lord.

Please write and share your experience with me (see contact address at the back of the book)

Chapter 4

The Next Step

Immediately following my 'born-again' experience I was greatly exercised to be baptized in water. This came about through regularly studying the Scriptures, particularly the New Testament. Almost every reading I considered contained the subject of water baptism. I was to learn at an early age in Christ that God often personally speaks in this way.

A divine command

As I gave the subject more serious consideration I realized that water baptism was a divine command not simply an option. And because I fervently desired to please the Lord in every area of my new 'born-again' experience I studied the subject more intensely.

I will point out that no human agency was involved in my final decision. I consented to be baptized because this was a divine and biblical command to be carried out to the praise and glory of God. My initial scriptural study revealed how the

Lord Jesus was baptized in the River Jordan at Bethabara by John the Baptist when our Lord was **thirty years of age**. Jesus was **an adult** when He was baptized in obedience to His Father, *'to fulfil all righteousness'* (Matthew 3:13–17; Luke 3:21–23). When our Lord was **a baby** eight days old He was **dedicated** to God in the temple at Jerusalem.

This solved a problem for me. I was 'christened' as **a baby** and questioned whether I should be baptized as **an adult**. The Lord Jesus settled the issue by His own personal experience. If I was to become His true disciple then He must be my pattern in all matters. I must always obey the voice of my Good Shepherd and do His bidding at all times.

New Testament church and water baptism

The apostle Paul (former name Saul) was soundly converted on the road to Damascus (Acts ch. 9). Three days later, the obedient disciple Ananias baptized Paul in water. During the convicting preaching of evangelist Philip in Samaria many were converted to Christ and were promptly baptized. The apostle Peter on the day of Pentecost commanded the convicted congregation:

> *'**Repent, and be baptized every one of you** in the name of Jesus Christ for the remission of sins, and ye shall receive the gift of the Holy Ghost. For the promise is unto you, and to your children, and to all that are afar off, even **as many as the Lord our God shall call**.'*　　　(Acts 2:38–39)

There is no doubting that the early Christians were promptly baptized in water at our Lord's command. The original Greek word *'baptizo'* means 'to immerse, to dip into', suggesting to be submerged beneath the water, if only briefly. Water baptism in this context spiritually implies 'dying to the old selfish carnal life' and 'rising in the newness of the Christ life'. An outward testimony to the inward change of heart.

Baptism by immersion

The biblical record of Christ's baptism strongly hints that Jesus was immersed and not simply doused with water. John the Baptist conducted his operations at Bethabara in the River Jordan. Here the river was deeper and flowed more slowly as it entered the Dead Sea a little way down. John baptized where *'there was much water'* (John 3:23).

The apostle Paul referring to Israel's miraculous crossing of the Red Sea uses this event to illustrate the true method of water baptism (see 1 Corinthians 10:1–2). The Israelites were commanded to go into and through the Red Sea and as they obeyed the waters heaped up on either side. They passed through the parting of the waters like unto an act of water baptism. This remarkable action separated them from the old life with the Egyptians and launched them into a new life en route to the Land of Promise. There is every scriptural evidence that true water baptism is by immersion.

I fellowshipped with a devout and dedicated company of Christians following my 'born-again' experience. When I shared with them my desire to be baptized they were most obliging and arranged a special service for the occasion. Having obeyed the Lord I was filled with unspeakable joy and my Christian experience was charged with renewed spiritual zeal and vision.

Have you been baptised?

I commend all new Christians to seriously consider Christ's command to be baptized:

> 'Go ye therefore, and teach all nations, **baptizing them** in the name of the Father, and of the Son, and of the Holy Ghost: Teaching them to observe **all things whatsoever I have commanded you:** and, lo, I am with you alway, even unto the end of the world. Amen.'   (Matthew 28:19–20)

Finally, Jesus issues this divine challenge to all Christians:

> 'If ye love me, keep my commandments.'
>   (John 14:15)

Prove your love for Christ and be baptized at His command.

Chapter 5

Receiving the Holy Spirit

Three months following my 'born-again' experience I received notice to join the Royal Air Force. I was to serve twenty-two months of national service. My first night in the barrack room proved a real test of my new-found faith in Jesus. The Lord stood by me, however, and I overcame my fears but recognized my ongoing need of God's anointing, power, and strength.

As I sought the Lord's response to my problem the Holy Spirit directed me to the book of Acts. I perceived how God had empowered the disciples of Jesus during a mighty and awesome visitation of the Holy Spirit. Among the waiting apostles in Jerusalem on the day of Pentecost was Peter who had denied his association with Jesus three times. There was Thomas noted for his unbelief and lack of faith. There were the sons of Zebedee rebuked by Jesus for having desired fire from heaven to consume their opponents. To these needy disciples, with their shortcomings and failings, Jesus promised Holy Spirit power from heaven.

A remarkable event

According to Acts, chapter 2, God responded in an unprecedented manner:

> *'And when the day of Pentecost was fully come, they were all with one accord in one place. And suddenly there came a sound from heaven as of a rushing mighty wind, and it filled all the house where they were sitting. And there appeared unto them cloven tongues like as of fire, and it sat upon each of them. And they were all filled with Holy Ghost, and began to speak with other tongues, as the Spirit gave them utterance.'* (Acts 2:1–4)

This awesome visitation of the Holy Spirit made a dramatic impact upon the apostles. They were immersed in the power of God. Charged with divine boldness they fearlessly preached the gospel with courage and conviction, their previous faults and failings completely overcome by the sanctifying influence of the Holy Spirit.

As I studied this event I knew this to be the answer to my problem. From that hour I sought the Lord with all my heart to be filled and sanctified by the Holy Spirit. Three weeks later, alone in the barrack room, I was blessed beyond words when God graciously baptized me with the Holy Spirit. My entire being flooded with heaven-sent glory. Rivers of living water poured into my thirsty soul. My tongue burst forth with heavenly languages. I was saturated in the power of God. From that blessed visitation my Christian life was completely transformed.

Have *you* received the Holy Ghost?

Reader, have you been filled with the Holy Spirit **since** you believed?

Some teach that we receive the Holy Spirit at our conversion, not as a separate or distinct experience. Turn to the book of Acts, chapter 9 and you will discover the scriptural record of the apostle Paul's experience. Without question, Paul was soundly converted on the Damascus highway and yet three days later he received the Holy Spirit under the hands of Ananias (Acts 9:17). A similar situation arose when Philip the evangelist preached with miraculous evidence in Samaria. Many were converted to Christ and Philip baptized them in water. The evangelist must have been thoroughly convinced they were genuine converts before he would baptize them. Yet **some time later** Philip requested Peter and John to come from Jerusalem to introduce the new Samaritan Christians to the Holy Spirit. They received the Holy Spirit as a separate and distinct experience from their 'born-again' experience (Acts 8:17).

Christ receives the Holy Spirit

The Lord Jesus received the blessed Holy Spirit following His baptism in the River Jordan. The heaven opened and the Holy Spirit came upon Him like a beautiful heavenly dove. Empowered from on high Jesus entered His ministry of preaching and healing. At that time our Lord was about **thirty years of age** (Luke 3:21–23). The 'born-again' experience is accomplished when the Holy

Spirit overshadows us and implants within our lives the incorruptible seed of the Christ life. Prior to this miraculous event the Holy Spirit convicts of sin and when we sincerely repent He guides us to the Saviour Jesus Christ. At conversion we receive the Christ nature, the Christ life within our lives.

Paul explains this when he states:

> *'Now if any man have **not** the **spirit of Christ** he is none of his.'*
>
> (Romans 8:9; see also 1 Peter 1:11)

Paul distinctly speaks here of the **Spirit of Christ** – i.e. **the nature and life of Christ – as distinct from the Person of the Holy Spirit. The Holy Spirit is the third Person** of the Godhead. He is a **person not** merely an influence or some abstract spirit being. During the 'born-again' experience we receive the **Christ life**. This divine impartation enables us to become like Jesus. When we receive the Holy Spirit we are divinely equipped for ministry, service and personal empowerment (Acts 1:8).

Reader, have you received **Christ**?

Have you **also** received the Holy Spirit since you believed?

The apostle Paul challenged the disciples at Ephesus with the same question:

> *'Have ye received the Holy Ghost **since** ye believed? And they said unto him, **We have not so much as heard whether there be any Holy Ghost.'***
>
> (Acts 19:2)

Note carefully – Paul questioned *'since you believed'* **not** 'when you believed'. In other words the Ephesians were genuine believers but had not received the Holy Spirit.

> *'And when Paul had laid his hands upon them, the Holy Ghost came on them; and they spake with tongues and prophesied. And all the men were about twelve.'* (Acts 19:6–7)

The Ephesian believers received the Holy Spirit as a separate and distinct experience to their 'born-again' conversion.

The divine evidence

It is also interesting to note the divine evidence that accompanied the receiving of the Holy Spirit. On the day of Pentecost the disciples *'were all filled with the Holy Ghost, and began to speak with other tongues as the Spirit gave them utterance'* (Acts 2:4).

When Cornelius and his household were filled with the Holy Ghost under the apostle Peter's ministry, *'they heard them speak with tongues, and magnify God'* (Acts 10:46).

The men at Ephesus also *'spake with tongues, and prophesied'* (Acts 19:6).

When Peter and John responded to Philip's call to the laying on of hands for the Samaritans to receive the Holy Spirit (Acts 8:17) there is every indication they also spake with tongues and prophesied because Simon was intrigued by the supernatural evidence he witnessed (read Acts 8:16–18).

Why should it be thought impossible for the Holy Spirit to operate in similar manner today? The

Holy Spirit continues to convict of sin, guide the sincere believer and empower the weak Christian, so we can expect to see other manifestations recorded in the Holy Scriptures. How dare we limit the ministry of the Holy Spirit by our narrow-minded theories and traditional ideas. If it was possible then, it is possible now!

Millions of believers world-wide have experienced the same Holy Spirit manifestations recorded in the book of Acts. Countless numbers of sincere Spirit-filled Christians have spoken in tongues and prophesied. The divine promise through the Apostle Peter at Pentecost *'even as many as the Lord our God shall call'*, certainly includes the Christians of this generation.

Reader, the Holy Scriptures assure you beyond question, the Holy Spirit is ready and willing to fill your life with heaven's grace and glory.

Contact me for further information (see address at the back of the book).

Chapter 6

Changed into His Image

In simple language, what is meant by 'being changed into God's image'? How do we analyse the process of becoming the sons of God? What evidence should be forthcoming?

The Holy Scriptures provide the answers to these intriguing questions. The nature and character of Jesus is set forth in Galatians chapter 5 under the heading **'the fruit of the Spirit'**.

> *'But the fruit of the Spirit is **love, joy, peace, longsuffering, gentleness, goodness, faith, meekness, temperance:** against such there is no law.'*
> (Galatians 5:22–23)

As we carefully analyse the exquisite nature of Jesus we discover that He manifested these nine listed fruits of the Spirit.

Love

Love is an outstanding aspect of God's divine nature, perfectly projected through the life of Christ. Jesus was moved with compassion when

He saw the multitudes and He healed their sick (Matthew 14:14). Our Lord wept with compassion at the tomb of Lazarus (John 11:35). Jesus so loved the world that He willingly laid down his life to secure our salvation:

> *'Greater love hath **no man** than this, that a man lay down his life for his friends.'* (John 15:13)

(Also read 1 Corinthians ch. 13.)

Joy

Jesus continued to experience divine joy in the face of persecution, crucifixion, and death.

> *'Looking unto Jesus the author and finisher of our faith; who for the **joy** that was set before him endured the cross, despising the shame, and is set down at the right hand of the throne of God.'*
> (Hebrews 12:2)

Jesus **delighted** to do the will of His Father – Our Lord sang a hymn before proceeding to Gethsemane (Matthew 26:30).

Peace

Christ is the Prince of Peace. Jesus shared His peace with His disciples.

> *'My peace I give unto you.'* (John 14:27)

Crossing the turbulent waters of Galilee, Jesus commanded *'peace be still'* (Mark 4:39) and the storm ceased. When Jesus suddenly appeared among His disciples following His resurrection, he declared *'My peace I give unto you'* (John 14:27), calming their fears . Jesus spoke peace to the troubled soul, the fear-filled heart and the disturbed mind.

Longsuffering

> *'The Lord is not slack concerning his promise, as some men count slackness; but is longsuffering to us-ward, not willing that any should perish, but that all should come to repentance.'*
>
> (2 Peter 3:9)

God's patience is enduring. It may stretch across many years to reach a lost soul with salvation. Never let up praying for the salvation or restoration of your loved ones, however far away from the Lord they may be.

Gentleness

At mother's knee a child could pray:

> Gentle Jesus meek and mild
> Look upon a little child.
> Suffer my simplicity
> Help me Lord, to come to Thee.

The apostle Paul reminds the church at Corinth of the gentleness of Christ (2 Corinthians 10:1). King David testifies, *'thy gentleness hath made me great'* (Psalm 18:35). Gentleness is a divine virtue attributed to the mighty God of creation. Humility and meekness join hands with gentleness.

Goodness

God is good! Surely goodness and mercy shall follow us all the days of our life (Psalm 23:6).

'The earth is full of the goodness of the LORD.'
(Psalm 33:5)

'The goodness of God endureth continually.'
(Psalm 52:1)

It is the goodness of God that leads us to repentance. Truly, God is a good God!

Faith

Jesus is the author and finisher of our faith. By grace we are saved, through faith, and that **not of ourselves**, it is **a gift from god** (Ephesians 2:8–9). Paul lived by the faith of Jesus Christ (Galatians 2:20). The disciples of Jesus earnestly requested, *'increase our faith'* (Luke 17:5).

Meekness

Meekness suggests modesty and deference, humbleness of mind and spirit. Christ's meekness is clearly reflected in His complete submission to the will of His Father. However, meekness does not imply weakness. Christ's strong condemnation of religious hypocrisy clearly indicates this.

Temperance

Temperance means moderation, involving self-control and abstinence. Jesus was a perfect example of self-discipline. Subject to constant abuse and false accusation He refused to lose His temper. He could have called legions of angels to His rescue but chose to go as a lamb to the slaughter without opening His mouth.

These nine fruits of the Spirit comprise the perfect nature of Jesus. We inherit these by abiding in

Christ. As the branch abides in the vine it will bring forth much fruit. We are known for our fruit-bearing. Our lives must radiate the fruit of the Sprit at all times.

Prayerfully consider the above listed nine fruits of the Spirit.

Seriously meditate upon their potential in your life. Consider your personal development of these virtues.

If you are failing in some measure ask the Lord to perfect the virtues lacking in substance.

Be determined to pursue the perfect operation of the fruit of the Spirit in your life.

As you continually abide in Christ the Holy Spirit will assist you to pursue and attain maturity.

We are called to be fully-fledged sons of God reflecting the image of the Lord.

Chapter 7

The Ministry of Gifts

As the **nine fruits of the Spirit** constitute the divine nature and character of Jesus so the **nine gifts of the Spirit** constitute His divine ministry. These Holy Spirit gifts are listed in 1 Corinthians, chapter 12.

> 'Now there are diversities of gifts, but the same Spirit. And there are differences of administrations, but the same Lord. And there are diversities of operations, but it is the same God which worketh all in all. But the manifestation of the Spirit is given to every man to profit withal. For to one is given by the Spirit the **word of wisdom**; to another the **word of knowledge** by the same Sprit; to another **faith** by the same Spirit; to another the **gifts of healing** by the same Spirit; to another the **working of miracles**; to another **prophecy**, to another **discerning of spirits**; to another **divers kinds of tongues**; to another the **interpretation of tongues**: But all these worketh that one and selfsame Spirit, dividing to every man severally as he will.' (1 Corinthians 12:4–11)

These nine gifts were manifested in the matchless ministry of Christ.

Word of wisdom

The **wisdom** of Jesus astonished many as He preached and reasoned with the people.

> 'And it came to pass, when Jesus had ended these sayings, the people were astonished at his doctrine: For he taught them as one having authority, and not as the scribes.' (Matthew 7:28–29)

The apostle Paul writes of Christ, 'the power of God, and the **wisdom** of God' (1 Corinthians 1:24). 'In whom are hid all the treasures of **wisdom** and knowledge' (Colossians 2:3).

When the officers of the chief priests failed to bring Jesus into captivity their excuse was, **'Never man spake like this man'** (John 7:46).

A classic example of the **word of wisdom** is recorded by St Matthew. The Pharisees attempting to entangle Jesus asked Him, 'Is it lawful to give tribute unto Caesar, or not?' (Matthew 22:17). Jesus perceived their wickedness and requested a penny.

> 'And he saith unto them, Whose is this image and superscription? They say unto him, Caesar's. Then saith he unto them, Render therefore unto Caesar the things which are Caesar's; and unto God the things that are God's. When they had heard these words, they marvelled, and left him, and went their way.' (Matthew 22:20–22)

Word of knowledge

Jesus also manifested the **word of knowledge**.

St John records how *'Jesus saw Nathanael coming to him, and saith of him, **Behold an Israelite indeed, in whom is no guile!'** (John 1:47).* Christ's analysis of Nathanael's character was given by divine revelation and declared in truth. Another intriguing occasion occurred when our Lord instructed two of His disciples to go into the city of Jerusalem and prepare the passover. Jesus gave knowledgeable indication that a man bearing a pitcher could surely guide them to the precise location. It came to pass exactly as Jesus described.

Faith

No one excelled more than Jesus with respect to **faith**. His impeccable trust in His Father could not be questioned. Little wonder His disciples earnestly requested more faith. I distinctly remember facing an impossible situation during my Indian crusades.

My faith wavered and I called upon the Lord for more faith. The Holy Spirit directed me to Galatians 2:20. I knew from that time I had ongoing access to the faith of the Son of God.

Gifts of healing

Jesus went about doing good and healing all manner of sickness and disease. Without question He manifested **the gifts of healing**, Christ Himself being the divine healer and physician. According to Hebrews 13:8, Jesus Christ is the same yesterday and today and forever. His healing ministry remains with us today and He continues to channel His healing grace through the **gifts of healing**. The specific use of the plural (**gifts** of healing) could suggest diversity of operations involving mind, spirit and body.

Working of miracles

Great multitudes followed Jesus when they saw His miracles. The first miracle was witnessed at Cana in Galilee where Jesus turned the water into wine. Probably His most outstanding miracle was the raising to life of Lazarus of Bethany four days after his death. Personally I have witnessed a number of miracles from Jesus during my fifty years of missionary ministry.

> Please request my book *Miracles* (see contact address at the back of this publication).

Prophecy

Christ's intimate knowledge of the future proved irrefutable. His detailed description of the destruction of Jerusalem in Matthew 24 is a masterpiece of forthtelling. Although the event did not take place until 37 years later, His accurate details were fulfilled to the letter.

Jesus also gave a graphic prediction of His suffering and crucifixion.

> *'I am the good shepherd: the good shepherd giveth his life for the sheep.'* (John 10:11)

> *'... and I lay down my life for the sheep.'* (John 10:15)

> *'The Son of man ... shall be delivered unto the Gentiles, and shall be mocked, and spitefully*

entreated, and spitted on: And they shall scourge
him, and put him to death: and the third day he
shall rise again.'   (Luke 18:31–33)

Loyal and faithful prophets appeared throughout
the Old Testament era but Jesus outshone them all.

Discerning of spirits

Our Lord also possessed the ability to **discern**
spirits – an essential factor in the casting out of
demons.

Divers kinds of tongues and interpretation

There is also sufficient evidence in the New Testament that Jesus had command of languages
including Greek, Hebrew and Aramaic. Most probably His divinity would allow Him to understand
languages and interpret them. When the Holy Spirit
fell upon the disciples at Pentecost they were able to
speak with other tongues and magnify God (Acts 2).

Many years after the Pentecostal outpouring the
apostle Paul dedicated an entire chapter of his first
epistle to the Corinthians to spiritual instruction
concerning the gifts of tongues, prophecy and the
interpretation of tongues. Carefully consider the
chapter 14 of Paul's epistle noting how all things
must be done decently and in order. Paul also
added:

'. . . and forbid not to speak with tongues.'
                        (1 Corinthians 14:39)

'I thank my God, I speak with tongues more than
ye all.'   (1 Corinthians 14:18)

45

Paul was **not present at Pentecost**, having received his spiritual gifts during a later period.

An ongoing experience of the indwelling Holy Spirit guarantees a permanent outworking of the fruit and gifts of the Spirit. Being constantly filled with the Spirit of God will enable us to face every situation with divine confidence. The fruit and gifts are the outward manifestation of the indwelling Holy Spirit. Thirst for and desire with all your heart to remain filled and controlled by the blessed Spirit of the living God.

Chapter 8

Relationship and Service

Genuine born-again Christians continually seek to deepen their relationship with the Lord. This must always be the first consideration. Our Lord's relationship with the Father provides an excellent example. Jesus and His Father lived and acted in perfect harmony.

Jesus said:

> *'I and my Father are one.'* (John 10:30)

This unique oneness evolved from our Lord's complete and total dependence upon the Father and His uncompromising love for His Father. The following statements from Jesus prove this:

> *'Verily, verily, I say unto you, The Son can do nothing of himself, but what he seeth the Father do.'* (John 5:19)

> *'My doctrine is not mine, but his that sent me.'* (John 7:16)

(See also John 5:30, 6:57 and 12:49.)

How easy to become self-sufficient and act independently of the Lord. To be self-motivated and self-confident. Some Christians shipwreck their experiences upon the proud rocks of self-projection. Others concentrate far more upon ministry, service and action than deepening their personal relationship with God. We can quickly lose sight of Jesus and be derailed through self-glorification. When this occurs, Christians lose their radiancy and anointing. We must never, never lose contact with Jesus.

Enriching our relationship

A born-again Christian's relationship with the Lord is deepened and enriched through love, dedication and obedience. We are commanded to love the Lord with all of our heart, soul, mind, and strength. God places this divine command at the top of our agenda. We express our love through worship, praise and fervent devotion. Such actions are precious to the Lord. Making melody in our hearts, rendering songs of gratitude and continually saying 'I love you Lord' is gratifying to the God of our salvation.

Implicit obedience is also an essential factor in deepening our relationship with Jesus. Jesus said:

'If ye love me, keep my commandments.'

John 14:15)

Obeying Christ is love in action. We must at all times respond to the voice of the Good Shepherd. We are the sheep of His pasture, under His care and oversight. Christ is also the Head of the Church, which is His body (Ephesians 1:22–23). We are members of His body. Born-again Christians are duty bound to obey Christ the Head of the Church. We should always be subordinate to the Head of the body. Sadly today, some Christians are taking more notice of man-made dogmas, schemes and ideas.

The original apostles of Christ never dictated nor organized other Christians but simply acted in an advisory capacity as God gave them wisdom. Jesus strongly opposed those who propagated the Nicolaitane doctrine (Revelation 2:6). Our priority responsibility is to hear and obey the voice of the Master.

Seek first God's Kingdom

The present-day church contains many Marthas – good folk who are so taken up with the mortal things of this life but have little time to sit at the feet of Jesus. Jesus said,

> *'Seek ye first the kingdom of God, and his right-eousness* [relationship]*; and all these things shall be added unto you.'* (Matthew 6:33)

Mary would sit at the feet of Jesus and listen to His voice. She drank at the fountain of eternal wisdom and partook of heaven's bread of life.

Mary chose the better part by deepening her relationship with Christ. Within this God-ordained relationship, the Lord has promised and guaranteed His continuing and abiding presence.

> *'Lo, I am with you alway, even unto the end of the world.'* (Matthew 28:20)

'My presence shall go with thee, and I will give thee rest.' (Exodus 33:14)

*'The L*ORD* is nigh unto all them that call upon him, to all that call upon him in truth.'*

(Psalm 145:18)

Faith and feelings

I recall the joy and excitement that resulted from my 'born-again' experience. My emotions were 'sky high'. Gradually, over some weeks the excitement faded and I began to wonder if the Lord had forsaken me. When I shared my dilemma with Jesus He graciously informed me:

'My Son, I am weaning you away from the **sense evidence** of My presence to the **Word-based evidence** of My presence. **hold fast to My promises not your feelings**.'

I was to remember this truth throughout my walk with the Lord. My faith must be rooted in God's Word not in my emotional feelings. I must walk by faith and not by sight (2 Corinthians 5:7).

'Blessed are they that have not seen, and yet have believed.' (John 20:29)

God says it, I believe it and that settles it!

The blood of Jesus

Every born-again Christian makes mistakes. I remember my first transgression following my conversion. This troubled me greatly. Once again I appealed to the Lord. Through this event I was to learn that the precious blood of Jesus Christ cleanses us from all sin.

> *'If we confess our sins, he is faithful and just to forgive us our sins, and to cleanse us from **all unrighteousness.'*** (1 John 1:9)

> *'If we walk in the light, as he is in the light, we have fellowship with one another, and the blood of Jesus Christ his Son cleanseth us from **all sin.'***
> (1 John 1:7)

I learnt to keep short accounts with God by promptly confessing my sins and seeking God's grace to live in victory over sin. Peace returned to my disturbed heart as heaven witnessed to my sincerity. I thank God, with profound appreciation, for the ongoing provision of the blood of Jesus to keep me pure and clean in heart and mind enabling me to commune and fellowship with the Lord throughout my days. Service for Christ must spring from our relationship with Christ. Abiding in Christ must precede our ministry for Christ.

Jesus said,

> *'Abide in me, and I in you. As the branch cannot bear fruit of itself, except it abide in the vine; no more can ye, except ye abide in me.'*
> (John 15:4)

> *'For without me you can do nothing.'*
> (John 15:5)

It is a privilege to serve the Lord whatever our calling.

Always pleasing God

Jesus did not view His ministry as an added duty or responsibility. He always identified service with the will of His Father.

> 'For I came down from heaven, not to do mine own will, but the will of him that sent me.'
>
> (John 6:38)

Our Lord's ministry evolved from His ongoing relationship with his Father. Jesus said,

> 'I do **always those things** that please him.'
>
> (John 8:29)

He also added that He **delighted** to do His Father's will (Psalm 40:8). Likewise the ministry of the born-again Christian must evolve from relationship with God. As we abide in Christ, the true Vine, our service and ministry will bear fruit. We must never operate independently of God's wisdom, grace, and power.

Jesus calls and ordains

Without God's direction, power and anointing we can do nothing to glorify the Lord and exalt His Holy Name. We can maintain a humble status, however, if we constantly recall the words of Jesus:

> 'Ye **have not chosen me, but I have chosen you**, and ordained you, that you should go and bring forth fruit, and that your fruit should remain.'
>
> (John 15:16)

It is **Christ** who calls, chooses, and ordains. Jesus never asked for volunteers. The Lord calls and appoints His apostles, prophets, evangelists, pastors, and teachers.

> *'And he* [Jesus] *gave some, apostles; and some, prophets; and some, evangelists; and some, pastors and teachers; for the perfecting of the saints, for the work of the ministry, for the edifying of the body of Christ.'*   (Ephesians 4:11–12)

Notice: '**Jesus gave**'. The Lord calls and appoints!

I wonder how many today, in Christian service, have been genuinely called by the Lord? Our church system alone cannot produce genuine God-ordained ministers. Simply filling our minds with theological and religious knowledge does not guarantee a genuine call of God. Gladys Aylward, the famous Chinese missionary, fell far short of men's expectations but she responded to a genuine call from God to faithfully labour in China for many years to the glory of the Lord.

Consult the Lord

Before rushing out into service seek the perfect mind and will of God. Elijah stood before the Lord before launching out into ministry. Jesus consulted His Father before going into action. We must be guided and directed at all times by the Spirit of the living God.

> *'For as many as are **led by the Spirit of God**, they are the sons of God.'*   (Romans 8:14)

We are called and ordained to serve the Lord. We are to listen to God's voice and do His bidding. When the apostles were commanded by the religious authorities to cease preaching and teaching in the Name of Jesus:

> 'Peter and John answered and said unto them, Whether it be right in the sight of God to hearken unto you more than unto God, judge ye. For we cannot but speak the things which we have seen and heard.' (Acts 4:19–20)

The faithful apostles first and foremost obeyed the voice of the Lord. Genuine sons of God are guided and directed by the Spirit of God. To know and understand the **mind** and **will of God** seek the Lord with all your heart. Wait before Him until He gives clear direction. Consult His Word for illumination and revelation. And always remember my favourite saying:

'Where God guides He always provides.'

Listen to the Lord and trust in the Lord with all your heart.

Chapter 9

Three Tests of Sonship

When God said, *'Let us make man in our image, after our likeness'*, He must have envisaged the perfect creation. Adam came close to this but in the hour of temptation failed the test. Where Adam failed, Jesus triumphed!

Beholding Christ we see the perfect Son, the unique prototype, the divine pattern, the end-product of God's golden vision. Take a long lasting look at Jesus. All true sons of God will eventually be fashioned after His glorious image and likeness.

God is patiently working to this golden end just like a carpenter patiently fashioning an exquisite piece of furniture.

As I behold Jesus, three unusual aspects of His life attract my attention.

First, His total and complete reliance upon His Father. Consider these sayings:

> *'Verily, verily, I say unto you, The Son **can do nothing of himself, but what he seeth the Father do**: for what things soever he doeth, these also doeth the Son likewise.'* (John 5:19)

'For as the Father hath life in himself: so hath he given to the Son to have life in himself.'
(John 5:26)

When the Jews marvelled at our Lord's sayings, He replied:

'My doctrine is not mine, but his [Father] *that sent me.'*
(John 7:16)

'As the living Father hath sent me, and I live by the Father . . . '
(John 6:57)

'For the Father loveth the Son, and sheweth him all things that himself doeth.'
(John 5:20)

Jesus relied upon His Father for guidance, wisdom, knowledge, understanding and revelation.

*'And he that sent me is with me: the Father hath not left me alone; **for I do always those things that please him**.'*
(John 8:29)

Likewise, the elected sons of God must learn to rely upon the Father. Instead of striving and struggling to fulfil the will of God with human effort and ingenuity they must rely upon the blessed Spirit residing within.

'Not by might, nor by power, but by my spirit, saith the LORD of hosts.'
(Zechariah 4:6)

Secondly, Christ's complete confidence in the Father eradicated all self-effort and self-motivation. Jesus knew that man's greatest problem lay within – the projection of self.

> *'For to be carnally* [selfishly] *minded is death; but to be spiritually minded is life and peace.'*
>
> (Romans 8:6)

> *'So then they that are in the flesh cannot please God.'* (Romans 8:8)

Christ died on the cross to settle the **sin problem and the self problem**. The root of the **sin problem** is the **carnal or self-nature**.

> *'But ye* [genuine sons of God] *are not in the flesh, but in the Spirit, if so be that the Spirit of God dwells within you.'* (Romans 8:9)

Jesus lived, served and ministered to please the Father, **never to please Himself**. Never once was He self-motivated or self-projected. His delight was to accomplish His Father's will:

> *'Then said I, Lo, I come: in the volume of the book it written of me, I delight to do thy will O, my God: yea, thy law is within my heart.'* (Psalm 40:7–8)

The sons of God will do likewise by dying to self and living in the power of God.

Thirdly, Jesus always glorified His Father. He accomplished all things for the glory of God. The glory of God is occasionally represented by **gold** in the Scriptures. The temple of Solomon contained numerous vessels of gold. These reflected the glory of God. Genuine, dedicated sons of God, go for gold! They fervently and consistently endeavour to glorify God in all they say and accomplish. They never glory in self or in man. They live to serve and please the Father. Their motives are always pure and God-glorifying. We must constantly examine our motives and attitudes. Are we seeking to please ourselves, exalt ourselves, project ourselves or seeking to exalt and glorify God? Are we going for gold or hay, wood and stubble? Are we pleasing men or pleasing God?

Jesus did always those things that pleased the Father. The sons of God must do likewise.

Chapter 10

Sonship in Reality

With God's sons nothing happens by chance or coincidence. Every situation and happening is part of the sonship maturing process. The Lord has the final word concerning everything that happens to His elected sons. Behind every situation there is a divine purpose and meaning. The apostle Paul understood this irrefutable truth when he wrote:

> 'And **we know** that all things work together for good to them that love God, to them who are **the called** according to His purpose.' (Romans 8:28)

When God's infallible Word says '**all**' He means '**all**'. Yes, **all** situations and circumstances are destined for our good.

Job's experience

Job's experience is a classic example. As we study Job's story we discover the following.

First, that nothing happens without God's permission. Satan could not touch Job until the Lord God had sanctioned it.

Secondly, the Lord allowed Job to be tested and tried for a divine purpose. In Job's case, the reason being, to bring to his notice a secret fear that had to be removed. This was part of Job's maturing process.

> *'For the thing which I greatly feared is come upon me, and that which I was afraid of is come unto me.'* (Job 3:25)

Thirdly, Job believed that 'good' would result from his severe trials and testings.

> *'But he knoweth the way that I take: when he hath tried me, I shall come forth as gold.'* (Job 23:10)

Finally, God honoured His promise to Job.

> *'So the LORD blessed the latter end of Job more than his beginning.'* (Job 42:12)

The heart of this divine process involved Job confessing his sin of fear and experiencing the Lord's deliverance.

> *'Wherefore I abhor myself, and **repent in dust and ashes**.'* (Job 42:6)

Consider God's counsel

The process of maturing into fully-fledged sons of God is not without testing by fire. Sometimes this may prove a very painful experience but the end product is golden and glorious. It is interesting to note, that at first, Job sought counsel and advice from his associates and friends. They offered various remedies and solutions to his problem. His wife suggested that he curse God and die. When Job sought **the Lord's** mind and understanding he responded positively:

> 'Curse God and die? **Never!** I'll **praise God and live.**'

How important to seek the Lord's answer rather than human counsel and advice. Genuine sons of God always do those things that please the Father.

Remember who you are

How easily we forget **who we are!** We quickly lapse into our carnal ways and lose sight of our high calling.

King Richard was known as the **'Lionheart'** because of his great courage and outstanding bravery. One day he faced the combined armies of five European nations. Seeing he was greatly out-numbered he decided to signal an orderly retreat. Whereupon his champion knight rode alongside to question this negative action:

'Have you ordered a retreat?' asked the knight.

'Yes,' replied Richard.

'Then, sire, **remember who you are!**'

King Richard recognizing that he had a name to live up to reversed the order and commanded an attack. Suddenly surprised by this change of tactics the opposing armies fled the battlefield and King Richard recorded a memorable victory.

Slaves no longer

The present-day sons of God face formidable foes. Satan and his hosts relentlessly attack the spirit, mind, and body. So it is essential for the sons of God to remember **who they are**. To remember they are no longer slaves of Satan but **sons of the living God**.

Never debate or argue with the works of the devil. Stand tall as a son of God and dislodge all evil in the Name of Jesus. Expel evil from every area of your life. Command it to flee in the invincible Name of Jesus.

- Never forget God is **with** you, for you, and **in** you!
- Cease retreating and launch an attack.
- Stop surrendering to doubt, worry and fear.
- Go on the offensive and fight the good fight of faith.
- Join the ever-expanding armies of the sons of God.
- If God be for you who dare stand against you?
- One with God is always a majority.
- One can put a thousand to flight; two can put ten thousands to flight.

This is the chosen hour for the sons of God to rise up and repel the works of darkness.

- Refuse to lie down and surrender.
- Cease retreating from the battlefield.
- You are more than conqueror through Christ who called you.
- Rise up, militant in purpose and strong in the Lord.
- Cast off the old garments of despair and put on the whole armour of God.

- Be strong in the Lord and the power of His might.

A daily confession

I frequently quote the following verses. Why not make them **your daily confession**?

A new creature

- I am a new creature, a new creation in Christ Jesus.
- I am born again, praise God, born from above.
- Old things have passed away and all things have become new.
- I am grafted into the Vine, the Lord Jesus.
- He is the Vine and I am the branch.
- I am a son of God, washed in His blood, born of His Spirit.
- I am glad I belong to Jesus.

- I am under new management. Jesus is my Lord and Master.
- I'm no longer a slave to sin and Satan. I've been set free.
- The Kingdom of God is within me.
- I am a temple of the Holy Ghost.
- Greater is Christ within me than the evil in the world.
- I am more than a conqueror through Christ who loves me.
- I can do all things through Christ who loves me.
- I can do all things through Christ who strengthens me.

Nothing too hard for God

- No weapon that is formed against me shall prosper.
- God is for me, who dare stand against me?
- The **Lord** is my refuge and strength whom shall I fear?
- God will always cause me to triumph.
- He will scatter my enemies from before me.
- There is nothing too hard for the Lord.
- His strength will overcome my weaknesses.
- He is my fortress and my stronghold.
- The Lord will preserve my going out and my coming in from this time forth.
- He is the strength of my life.
- I will resist the devil and he will flee from me.
- With Christ within victory is certain.

- This is the day that the Lord has made.
- I will rejoice in the Lord at all times.
- All things will work together for good for the Lord goes before me.
- He will direct my paths and guide me continually.
- He has put a new song in my heart.
- I have put on the garment of praise and will bless the Lord at all times.
- Nothing will silence my song of thanksgiving.
- The Lord's Name be praised! Now and always!
- With God all things are possible.
- There is nothing too hard for the Lord.
- Things impossible with men are possible with God.
- I will trust the Lord at all times.
- He will make a way where there is no way.

- He never slumbers nor sleeps.
- The Lord never changes! Jesus never fails!
- The God of miracles will always undertake for me therefore I will praise Him without ceasing.

Wonderful, wonderful Jesus!

Chapter 11

'Be Ye Perfect' Said Jesus

God, the Father, is fully committed to perfecting the sons He has called and saved. Every trial and testing is divinely designed to this purpose.

> '...that we may present every man **perfect** in Christ Jesus.' (Colossians 1:28)

God will test and perfect our **love** by allowing us to experience situations which would normally breed hatred or resentment. He will test and perfect our **joy** by placing us in depressing environments or among melancholy associates. He will likewise perfect our **patience** by slowing us down or delaying an answer to our prayers. Behind every divinely permitted situation God our Father is revealing His love and wisdom. Sadly, so often, the wisdom of this world flows from corrupt minds but the wisdom from above flows from the mind of our all-wise God.

Measuring our spirituality

But, how do the sons of God measure their maturing in Christ? How can you correctly assess your true spiritual status? How do you measure the depth of your spirituality?

One memorable Christmas time I was visiting a large shopping store. As I passed through the swing doors two excitable youngsters rushed by. They raced to a measuring scale erected to determine their natural heights. The young girl arrived first and promptly occupied the measuring scale only to be pushed aside by her younger brother.

'I've grown two inches,' claimed the lad.

'No, you haven't! I've grown two-and-a-half inches,' she retorted, determined not to be outdone by her brother.

The last I saw of them they were still arguing and debating.

An intriguing idea

This unique incident triggered an idea in my mind. Maybe we should consider a **measuring scale** so we could readily determine our **spiritual status in Christ**.

With many years of Christian experience I have come to one certain conclusion: that in order to determine my personal degree of spirituality I must sincerely assess how I **react to all of life's opposing situations**:

- How do I respond when falsely accused or encounter criticism and resentment?

- How do I react when my gifts and talents are despised by others?
- Am I willing to forgive those who despitefully use me?
- Do I love my enemies as Christ commanded?
- When under pressure do I panic or remain calm and peaceful?

Our reaction to opposing situations and difficult circumstances certainly makes a deep impact upon our spirituality. **What would Jesus do?** When faced with similar testings I endeavour to enquire of God:

- **'How would Jesus react?'**
- **'What would Jesus do?'**
- **'How would He handle the situation?'**

I have discovered that the Lord graciously responds to such sincere questions. God's **perfect Son, Jesus,** has all the answers. Jesus knows how to react to every complex problem. If we take time to listen to His counsel and advice we can react accordingly.

They say, 'live in close proximity to someone and you become like them.' How true this is of yourself and Jesus. Abide in ever closer communion with Christ and you will become like Him. Constantly fellowship with the Lord and sure enough you will be changed into His image. You will react to each trial and temptation in the Jesus way.

- You will **joy** in tribulation and laugh at impossibilities.
- You will love your enemies and pray for those who despitefully use you.

- You will respond to temptation with authority and power.
- You will resist the devil and he will flee from you.
- You will shed abroad the love of Jesus in ever-increasing quantities.

As with the disciples of old, the worldlings will take knowledge of you that you have been with Jesus. Hidden from view are our minds. Never has the mind been so subject to relentless attacks and onslaughts as in the present age.

The mind of Christ

Maturing sons of God must learn how to bring every thought into captivity to the **mind of Christ**.

> '*Let this mind be in you, which was also in Christ Jesus.*' (Philippians 2:5)

The thought life must be controlled and sanctified at all times. Pure and positive thoughts are vital to our spiritual health. Unclean and impure thoughts must be instantly rejected and promptly replaced by thoughts that are pure and clean. A righteous and peaceful mind is a major contribution to having the '**mind of Christ**'. In turn, having the **mind of Christ** is a major step in the pursuit of perfection.

The **worried mind** is harassed by fearful thoughts and forebodings. The **butterfly mind** flits from one subject to another, often out of control. The **over-active mind** is overwhelmed with tiring, restless thoughts that relentlessly pound the brain. The

obsessed mind is fixed on negative suggestions and sometimes lustful desires. The **mind of Christ** is the prize ambition of the true sons of God in the spiritual and moral quest for perfection.

Chapter 12

A Golden Occasion

One of the most remarkable events of all time will soon take place. The apostle Paul details this as follows:

> *'For the Lord himself shall descend from heaven with a shout with the voice of the archangel, and with the trump of God: and the dead in Christ shall rise first: then we which are alive and remain shall be caught up together with them in the clouds, to meet the Lord in the air: and so shall we ever be with the Lord. Wherefore comfort one another with these words.'*
>
> (2 Thessalonians 4:16–18)

The **in Christ** believers throughout the Church age will be gathered by the Lord and the holy angels into heaven. Our Lord's very own words predict this golden happening:

> *'And he shall send his angels with a great sound of a trumpet, and they shall gather together his elect from the four winds* [earth], *from one end of heaven (heaven) to the other.'*   (Matthew 24:31)

A dynamic impact

This outstanding and unprecedented occurrence will involve the Christians who have previously died and those who are living at the time of Christ's appearing. They will be changed and transformed by the mighty power of God, having miraculously experienced the dynamic impact of Christ's resurrection power. The Lord will appear from heaven and at the sound of the trumpet the dead in Christ will be raised incorruptible with new glorified bodies. Almost immediately the living **in Christ** will join them having likewise changed in a moment, in the twinkling of an eye. This united glorified company will appear in heaven as described by the apostle John in the Book of the Revelation:

> *'After this I beheld, and, lo, a great multitude, which no man could number, of **all nations, and kindreds, and people, and tongues**, stood before the throne, and before the **Lamb**, clothed with white robes, and palms in their hands: And cried with a loud voice, saying, **Salvation to our God** which sitteth upon the throne and unto the **Lamb**.'*
> (Revelation 7:9–10)

This amazing happening will rapidly accelerate **God's golden vision**. Following years of subjection to the devastating laws of **sin** and **death**, the redeemed company will be miraculously unshackled and emancipated from the chains of bondage and ushered triumphantly into the presence of God.

An unprecedented scene

For an allotted span of time they will show their profound gratitude to God with pure worship and songs of thanksgiving. Having been washed in the blood of the Lamb and sanctified by the Spirit of God they will wave their palms of praise before the throne.

Such an unprecedented scene will prove beyond human description. Like the sound of many waters the courts of heaven will resound with numerous soul-stirring anthems glorifying God. This divinely purposed period of glorification will be climaxed by the marriage supper of the Lamb.

> *'Let us be glad and rejoice, and give honour to him: for the marriage of the Lamb is come, and his wife hath made herself ready. And to her was granted that she should be arrayed in fine linen, clean and white: for the fine linen is the righteousness of saints. And he said unto me, Write, **Blessed are they which are called unto the marriage supper of the Lamb**. And he saith unto me, These are the true sayings of God.'*

(Revelation 19:7–9)

A new chapter dawns

This innumerable company of the redeemed will then accompany Christ, **the Word of God**, back to the earth to smite and overcome the enemies of the Lord.

> *'And I saw heaven opened, and behold **a white horse; and he that sat upon him was called***

Faithful and True, and in righteousness he doth judge and make war ... And the armies which were in heaven followed him upon white horses, clothed in fine linen, white and clean [redeemed saints].'
(Revelation 19:11, 14)

Zechariah, the Old Testament prophet, adds his inspired contribution:

*'For I will gather **all nations** against Jerusalem to battle; and the city shall be taken ... Then shall the* LORD *go forth and fight against those nations ... And **his feet shall stand in that day upon the mount of Olives ... and the** LORD **my God shall come, and all the saints with thee.**'*
(Zechariah 14:2, 3, 4, 5)

The returning Christ, accompanied by his saints and holy angels, will triumph over the forces of darkness. Satan will be cast into the bottomless pit and the earth will be purged of this evil for a thousand years.

The glory of the Lord will cover the planet earth like the waters cover the sea. A new chapter in the era of **God's golden vision** will have dawned.

Chapter 13

The Coming Golden Age

Every age and dispensation has its own particular design during which some certain divine intention is accomplished by the Lord. The coming golden age will witness Christ reigning and ruling on the earth with His saints alongside. During previous dispensations the foundation was laid and now the living temple will appear on earth. God does not build the building first and afterwards the foundation. He lays the foundation first and then builds the temple. He calls and appoints the sons of God first. Then He gives them dominion to rule and reign with Him as kings and priests on the earth.

The intention of God during the Church age is to call out an elect people, 'to take out a people for His name.' The coming golden age, the millennial kingdom, will enable the Lord to educate and perfect the sons of God into kings and priests. In other words the Church age is the 'calling out age' and the coming kingdom age will be 'the perfecting age for the sons of God'.

Christ with His regal power and authority will dwell and tabernacle with His glorified saints on earth for one thousand years teaching them to become fully-fledged sons of the living God.

The city of Jerusalem

During this new dispensational golden age the throne of David will be established in Jerusalem and upon it, Jesus the Son of David, will reign for a specific period of 1,000 years. His blessed kingdom will extend all over the earth and the **in-Christ** saints will reign with Him.

During this period Satan will be confined and his evil activities restrained. The earth will experience a peace so wonderful and complete. All wars will cease. All curses that now blight the earth will disappear. The glory of the Lord will cover the earth like the waters cover the sea.

One thousand years

Six times in Revelation chapter 20 the length of the coming golden millennial kingdom is definitely stated as 1,000 years. Some expositors have tampered with these figures but in spite of all the 1,000 years is of divine inspiration and will remain steadfast and sure. Until this point in time no human has lived on this earth beyond the age of 969 years. This time span was allotted to Methuselah for a special purpose. His name means 'when I die the judgment will come'. Methuselah died early in the year 1656 a few weeks prior to the 'pouring out of waters' upon the rebellious Noah society. God witnessed to a sinful world through the name Methuselah for over 900 years but they refused to listen to His merciful warning.

During the coming golden age the returning saints will live on the earth a full 1,000 years. A privilege reserved for the faithful.

The golden future

The prophet Isaiah reviewing the golden future predicts:

> *'Every valley shall be exalted, and every mountain and hill shall be made low: and the crooked shall be made straight, and the rough places plain: and the **glory of the Lord shall be revealed, and all flesh shall see it together**: for the **mouth of the Lord hath spoken it.**'*   (Isaiah 40:4–5)

Isaiah further predicts the coming of Christ endowed with wisdom and understanding to reprove and judge the world:

> *'When the Son of man shall come in his glory, and all the holy angels with him, then shall he sit upon the throne of his glory: and before him shall be gathered all nations: and he shall separate them one from another, as a shepherd divideth his sheep from the goats.'*   (Matthew 25:32)

Christ will judge the nations in righteousness and with divine authority:

> *'With righteousness shall he judge the poor, and reprove with equity for the meek of the earth:*

and he shall smite the earth with the rod of his
mouth, and with the breath of his lips shall he slay
the wicked.'   (Isaiah 11:4)

The animals transformed

An amazing transformation will take place within
the animal kingdom:

> *'The wolf also shall dwell with the lamb, and the*
> *leopard shall lie down with the kid; and the calf*
> *and the young lion and the fatling together; and **a***
> ***little child shall lead them**. And the cow and the*
> *bear shall feed; their young ones shall lie down*
> *together: and the lion shall eat straw like the ox.*
> *And the sucking child shall play on the hole of the*
> *asp, and the weaned child shall put his hand on*
> *the cockatrice den. **They shall not hurt nor***
> ***destroy in all my holy mountain**: for the earth*
> *shall be **full of the knowledge of the** Lord, as*
> *the waters cover the sea.'*   (Isaiah 11:6–9)

Read those verses again and grasp their amazing
significance.

Thy kingdom come

This is **the kingdom** foreseen by the holy prophets
as they were greatly inspired by the Spirit of God.
This is **the kingdom** we pray for each time we
repeat the Lord's prayer.

> *'Thy kingdom come. Thy will be done in earth, as*
> *it is in heaven.'*   (Matthew 6:10)

This is **the kingdom** in which Christ and the sons of God will reign for 1,000 years. **This kingdom** of the golden age like all other dispensations will fulfil its own particular purpose in the greater plan of God – making man in His own image and likeness.

Chapter 14

The End Time Drama

Once the dark clouds of judgment threatening this present dispensation have passed, Christ will return to this earth to reign supreme over the nations of the world. Zechariah, the Old Testament Prophet, gives a detailed prediction of this forthcoming event. He tells how the sacred city of Jerusalem will be surrounded by opposing nations rifling the houses, ravishing the women, and capturing half the city. And:

> *'Then shall the LORD go forth, and fight against those nations, as when he fought in the day of battle. And **his feet shall stand in that day upon the mount of Olives**, which is before Jerusalem on the east, and the **mount of Olives shall cleave in the midst thereof toward the east and toward the west**, and there shall be a very great valley ... and the LORD my God shall come, **and all the saints with thee.'***
>
> (Zechariah 14:3–5)

Jerusalem Under Attack

During the final drama of this dispensation when the city of Jerusalem faces certain defeat God will personally intervene. Jesus will appear on the **Mount of Olives** thus fulfilling the promise made by the two angels at Christ's ascension. The Lord will be accompanied by **all His saints** and an angelic host. Jesus adds His personal prediction of this traumatic event in the Book of Revelation.

> *'And I saw heaven opened and behold a **white horse**; and he that sat upon him **was called Faithful and True**, and in righteousness he doth judge and make war. His eyes were as a flame of fire, and on his head were many crowns; and he had a name written, that no man knew, but he himself. And he was clothed with a vesture dipped in blood: and his name is called **The Word of God**. And the **armies which were in** [from] **heaven followed him upon white horses, clothed in fine linen, white and clean** [saints, see verse 8]. And out of his mouth goeth a sharp sword, that with it he **should smite the nations; and he shall rule them with a rod of iron . . .** '*
> (Revelation 19:11–15)

Satan overcome

The returning **Christ** accompanied by **all His saints** and the holy angels will make war against the rebellious beast and kings of the earth.

> *'And the beast was taken, and with him the false prophet that wrought miracles before him, with*

84

> *which he deceived them that had received the mark of the beast, and them that worshipped his image. These both were cast alive into a lake of fire burning with brimstone.'*　(Revelation 19:20)

After the evil is subdued, Christ and His saints will reign upon the earth, and:

> *'Blessed and holy is he that hath part in the first resurrection: on such the second death hath no power, but they shall be priests of God and of Christ, and* **shall reign with him a thousand years***.'*　(Revelation 20:6)

The **golden era** will begin and God's **golden future will become a glorious reality**.

Chapter 15

God's Golden Future Extended?

John's amazing vision

At the end of the Kingdom Age the apostle John was privileged to see the fulfilment of God's golden future. He was transported by the Holy Spirit to a high mountain to preview one of the most spectacular scenes of all time. He witnessed the inerasable sight of the divinely designed new city of Jerusalem descending from heaven onto the new earth. Described as a living city, and compared with a virgin pure and holy, words fail to describe the intrinsic wonder of such heavenly glory. A city most beautiful and most holy adorned as a bride for her husband.

> *'And there came unto me one of the seven angels ... saying, Come hither, and I will shew thee **the bride**, the Lamb's wife. And he carried me away in the spirit to a great and high mountain, and*

> *shewed me that great city, the holy Jerusalem, descending out of heaven from God, having **the glory of God**; and her light was like unto a stone most precious, even like a jasper stone, clear as crystal.'* (Revelation 21:9–11)

This glorious city will descend from heaven at the end of the millennial kingdom. It will be the new capital of the new world. The nations of the earth will walk in the light of it and will bring their honour and glory into it. In the midst of it will stand the tree of life and the river of life will flow from the throne of God through the midst of it.

John dedicates the final two chapters of the Book of Revelation describing the unimaginable glory that will introduce the final instalment of God's golden vision.

The great voice

He tells of the great voice that will herald the arrival of the new holy city onto the new earth.

'The tabernacle of God is with men' (Revelation 21:3), the Lord Himself dwelling with them, living with them, residing with them. O, the wonder of it all. God in the midst of His people! How the disciples of Jesus must have rejoiced in the immediate presence of their Master. How they held fast to His every word and saying. How they bathed in the wonder and splendour of His nearness. And yet this supreme blessedness would prove just a foretaste of the indescribable experience of God tabernacling with His saints. Eye hath not seen, neither has it

entered into believing hearts what God hath prepared for them that love Him.

No more sorrow or pain

With God dwelling in the midst there will be no more sorrow, no more crying, no more pain or sickness. Death, the last stranglehold of Satan, will be no more. These former things will pass away. God will make all things new. The overcomers will inherit all things and God will be pleased to call them *'My sons'*. There will be no more curse. The curse of the earth, a direct result of the original fall, will be lifted. No more thorns and briars to blight the land. The curse of the law will cease as the nations walk in righteousness and obedience to the laws of the Lord. The redeemed, glorified saints will delight to walk in white and do always those things that please the Father. Transformed into God's image and likeness they will carry His Name in their foreheads.

The golden city

The new city of Jerusalem will be made of pure gold and garnished with all manner of precious stones. The wall of the city will comprise twelve foundations named after the twelve apostles of the Lamb. The twelve gates will be named after the twelve tribes of Israel and will comprise twelve exquisite pearls. The streets of the city will be of pure gold, as it were transparent glass. The city will lie four square and the length and breadth and height of it will be equal. Never again will sin, disease, death and rebellion rear their ugly head. The depravity of evil will be banished forever.

The river of life

The pure river of the water of life will flow through the midst of the holy city. On either side of the river the tree of life will flourish, bearing twelve kinds of fruit for the healing of the nations. There shall be no night there. No sun nor moon will shine. The light of God's glory will illuminate the city. The inhabitants will see His face and delight in His holy presence. The redeemed will stand in absolute awe before this amazing scene rendering unto God all honour, praise, and glory. Then, throughout all coming ages they will continue to love and adore the God of creation from whom all blessings flow.

- Will the God of creation extend His golden vision to other areas of the cosmos?
- Will He decide to transform the myriads of planets into inhabited worlds?

These are indeed intriguing questions only the God of creation can answer.

One thing is certain – **with God the future is golden**.

Chapter 16

Your Sonship Calling

The day you surrendered your life to Christ you were enrolled into your **sonship calling**. Like the prodigal son, you returned from the wilderness of sin to receive the Father's embrace and '**welcome home**'. Your garments were tattered and torn. The obnoxious smell of your past sinful life had to be removed. Jesus came to the rescue, saved you, and clothed you in His righteousness. A ring of authority was placed on your finger. New shoes adorned your feet and the Father celebrated your return by preparing the fatted calf.

You were so grateful to God for forgiving and receiving you that you were quite content to be a servant. You would have gladly served in the kitchen or some other menial task. Not so! The Father welcomed you home **as His son**. You were destined to **sonship *not* servitude**. You were called to be **a son of the living God**.

This is the **golden future God has in mind for you**!

The prize of sonship

The prize of **sonship** is a prize beyond the scope of human imagination. To be a **son of God** and a **joint heir** with Christ is a **golden hope** which defies all possibility of description.

When the apostle John spoke of sonship, he surrounded this blessed subject with the pure love of God:

> *'Behold, what manner of love the Father hath bestowed upon us, that we should be called the **sons of God** ... and it doth not yet appear what we shall be* [mature sons]*: but we know that, when he shall appear, we shall be like him; for we shall see him as he is. And every man that hath this hope in him purifieth himself even as he is pure.'*
> (1 John 3:1–3)

Your faith may stagger and falter at the possibility of becoming a mature son of God but **hope** smiles and cries 'it shall be done'. Hope is the forerunner of faith and hope will stimulate the burning desire to purify yourself even as Christ is pure. Hope delivers you from despair and failure.

> *'Hope thou in God: for I shall yet praise him, who is the health of my countenance, and my God.'*
> (Psalm 42:11)

The ongoing process

From the moment the blessed Spirit of God planted the divine seed of the Christ life within you, the process of **sonship** began. Your 'second birth' heralded the start of your new relationship with the Father.

> *'I will declare the decree: the LORD has said unto me, thou art my Son; this day have I begotten thee. Ask of me, and I shall give thee the heathen for thine inheritance, and the uttermost parts of the earth for thy possession.'*　　(Psalm 2:7–8)

These sacred verses are in direct harmony with those recorded in Genesis 1:26–28:

'And God said, Let us make man in our image, after our likeness: and let them have dominion ... over every living thing that moveth upon the earth.'

Fierce opposition

Satan will intensely oppose every step you take in pursuit of your sonship calling. He will try every subtle means to restrict your progress. He is a jealous adversary. Remember how he fiercely opposed Jesus in the wilderness and throughout His ministry. Nevertheless, **stand firm and resolute**. Your calling is from above. If God be for you who can stand against you?

- The Lord **will perfect that which concerns you**!
- Jesus triumphed! You **will triumph**!
- You **will** pass the test and graduate as a mature and perfect **son of God**.
- Jesus **will** present you spotless and faultless before the Father.

- He that hath begun this good work within you *will* **perform it**.
- Whatever the opposition, however testing the fiery furnace, the Lord *will* stand by you.

Put on the best robe. Stand in the righteousness of Christ. Wear the ring of delegated authority. Place the shoes on your feet and walk upright in the perfect **will of God**.

Refuse to be discouraged

Refuse to be discouraged when the way becomes difficult. See the end from the beginning. Set your heart and mind on **God's golden vision** and dare to believe your present and ongoing situation is divinely designed to ensure that you participate in **God's golden vision**.

It certainly is **through the boundless grace and love of God**.

To contact Peter Scothern, please write to:

Peter Scothern Ministries
PO Box 61
Gloucester GL4 3AA
England

(postage appreciated)